Beauty in The Journey

Cassandra Webb

Edited by: Mariko Irving

ISBN-13: 978-1-7322983-1-6
EireneBros Publishing LLC
4414 82nd St, Ste 212, -318
Lubbock, TX 79424
www.eirenebrospublishing.com
www.facebook.com/EireneBrosPublishing

Dedication

To my mother, for believing, supporting, and pushing me to write this book.

From the bottom of my heart, thank you.

Maria –
Thank you for
being my friend at
work. My day brightens
when I see you!

Contents

Cast your Anxieties on Me

Here you are, lying on your bed.

Thinking about everything you regret.

With the lights down....

With your Bible on the ground.

I know your pain;

I understand how you are feeling right now.

My beloved, I can help you through the pain.

But first, you need to come to me.

Cast your anxieties on me;

let ME take care of you.

When will you finally trust me-

the God who created you?

I love you more than the birds in the air.

I love you more than the fish in the sea.

Cast your anxieties on me

and I will take care of them for you.

Depression

Darkness seems to envelop me

suffocating me with every breath I take.

I know that this isn't the end,

but it seems like it's more than I can take.

I am searching for a door

that can take me anywhere but here.

But as soon as it seems like I find one,

it soon disappears.

So I sit down in this darkness,

waiting for it to finish its work.

Hoping that I can ride through it,

and hoping that I can find something that works.

Seems like nobody will understand,

even though some say they do.

But they don't know the pain

that I put myself through.

Outward vs. Inward

I have so many feelings.

It's hard to describe every single one.

Some are neutral,

and some are mutual;

it's hard to explain what's deep inside.

Though I may seem fun at times,

inside I am really hurting.

I just want you to hold me tight

and tell me everything's going to be alright.

Here I am

What do you see in me?

I am just a boy doing his duties.

I lay in your temple tonight

laying by the candlelight.

I hear someone calling me.

I don't know where it's coming from;

it's all around me.

When you reveal yourself to me:

Here I am!

For your servant is listening.

Here I am;

what do you want me to do?

Whatever be the price

I counted the cost and I know what's right.

I want to follow you.

Here I am.

What do you see in me?

I am just a girl doing her duties.

I lay in bed tonight

surrounded by the things that seem trivial in life....

When I Have Fears

When I have fears it is mostly about you.

The years we have never shared;

the father I will never look up to.

I thought you would actually care

about the daughter that you never knew.

I have hoped this idle hope,

but alas, this is not to be true.

The many tears I have shed.

Oh, how I wish it wasn't true!

And how my heart bled,

when I found out the truth.

It's too late to take back what you said.

When you have already done damage,

to a heart that you cannot bandage.

Forgiveness

When I had fears, it was the thought of meeting you.

Of a father

that I never once knew.

All of the hurt and the anger that I've

held for so long,

would they finally break through?

Would all of the hurting words I've wanted to say...

Would I have finally said them to you?

It took me a long time to come to acceptance;

to finally forgiving you.

All the broken promises and

your absence,

yes, I forgive you.

What good is holding a grudge when all it

does is tear you in two?

It's like a cancer

until it consumes you.

No, I may not understand why you chose the life

you live,

but that's ok too.

Healing doesn't come from the explained

All I can do is pray that one day

something will happen to make you turn your life

around

before it's too late.

To my Sister

Tired of feeling the sadness.

I'm tired of feeling the pain.

All the arguments we had all those nights,

they were pointless anyway.

Wish I could go back to the past;

take everything back and start it all new.

Words cannot express how much I miss you.

I wish I knew you for who you were,

and not the image of a daughter that sees her biological father.

But wishing will get us nowhere;

all it does is pour salt on a wound.

I am ready to restore our relationship

when you're ready to restore it too.

They say time heals all wounds,

but they never say how long the healing will take.

I can just hope that I won't be too late.

Just for You

Before I was hung, I knew what would come.

I knew I would give my life

just for you.

They made me carry the cross that was made by me,

for I made the trees in the forests.

They hung me with nails that murdered countless lives.

Each time I heard the hammer pounding, I thought of saving your life

so you wouldn't die in vain.

They placed the crown of thorns on my head

as blood poured down my face.

Every time they dropped on the ground,

I knew I would make you in your mother's womb.

They pierced me with a spear

That made you my sons and daughters.

Before I was hung, I knew what would come.

I knew I would give my life,

just for you.

When will the Heart?

Bang...Bang...Bang!

I pound on the steel barrier

that is around my heart.

"Why don't you let me in?

Can I just get a glimpse of what is going on

and try to help you?"

I hear nothing at first but then

I hear a soft whisper:

"I have tried letting you in

but you kept shutting me down.

I show you memories that hurt

but still, you will not bow

or get down on my level."

I stood in bewilderment,

helpless and so ashamed of myself.

"I'm sorry!" I cried out.

"It's the only thing I know how to do;

that and eat food to stuff the feelings away,

or start a new addiction to ease the pain."

I then hear a hurt voice full of emotion.

"Those aren't helping at all.

But keep eating and abusing me for all I care.

You don't love me at all! Leave me alone!"

I fall to my knees, my whole body heaving with sobs.

"I want to love you, but I don't know how!"

I then hear a still and peaceful voice:

"Why don't you trust me? The God who created you?"

I then say with so much hurt and anger,

"How do I know you aren't going to leave me? How do I know that you aren't going to hurt me like everyone else that came in and walked out of my life?

I don't believe you! I can't trust you!"

My head knows that this isn't true,

But when will my heart?

Confusion

I am running a race that seems so long.

Sometimes I lose the will to continue.

I lose hope, but yet, I know I have to move on.

Sometimes it seems I am missing something,

but I cannot put my finger on it.

Seems like I am just standing there,

not moving forward or back.

Seems like I have more stormy days;

More days where I reflect on what has happened to me in the past.

Where is the person I once knew?

Why can't I go back to who I was before I ended up here?

My mind goes around in circles and circles and circles and cir--

STOP!

I know I'm worthy to be loved.

I know that I have a purpose in life.

But why am I here?

Why am I so confused?

Cynical Soul

Heavy laden and weighed down, I walk this lonely road I've ever known.

What is love? This must be a myth;

something that I can only barely touch

before it runs away again.

Leaving me yearning and feeling more empty than before.

Will I come to know what it is?

Know what love between man and woman

is like before my life on this Earth ends?

I know I have many more years ahead;

many more miles to go before my eternal rest draws near.

Be still, my soul! Rest in the light of God's love;

God's amazing grace is sufficient for you.

He knows what he is doing and

You need to know that you do not.

What is Love?

I'm back in the desert place, longing for something more.

Where is the passion I once had?

Why do I have a thirsty soul?

These questions my heart ponders,

or subconscious, whichever it may be,

along with so many other questions.

I cannot put words to them all.

What is love?

Besides love from family and friends, what is this love

that I hear between a woman and her man?

I've had the taste of that wicked word Lust,

but it wasn't love at all.

Lust uses and makes a person BELIEVE it is love,

but it leaves a person empty; longing for something more.

Lust leaves a bad taste in the mouth;

it turns the attitude into something rotten.

It changes a person's view of the world,

and thinks there's motive behind an innocent's intent.

No...nothing good can come from lust, of that I am certain.

So...what is love?

The Knitter's Hands

Carefully and softly, I knitted you in your mother's womb.

I took my time counting the hairs on your head

and made you unique so that you wouldn't look like anyone else.

I carefully planned your future; I know the days your heart will be broken in two.

I also know the decisions that you will make that I will not approve.

I promise to be near you always.

Through the trials and the joys you will face in life.

I will guide you on the right path,

teaching you things and molding you into my likeness.

My beloved child,

no matter what you do,

I will always love you.

The Leper

I'm living on my own because no one wants to be near me.

Everyone says there is no hope for a cure for the disease of leprosy.

I see no hope in my future;

everything I did before is now just a fading memory. It was all meaningless.

The hours turn into days and the days turn into forever.

Then I heard about a man who can heal me of my disease.

It sounds too good to be true, but I go to him hoping.

Hoping that he holds the miracle of life.

I don't know what he will say.

He may reject me,

but I'm used to that anyway.

When I saw him coming, I yelled out my plea for healing.

What I saw shocked me.

His face was full of compassion for me.

When he hugged me, I was clean instantly!

I now have the joy I thought I would never know again.

I'm glad I was brave to go to him so he could cleanse me of my sin.

Arms of Comfort

Heartbroken and torn, I long to be held and comforted.

There are many ways to avoid the hurt and pain but I'm left longing for more.

Then without warning, you came to my side.

But I was scared for I have many sins to hide.

But you opened your arms of comfort and whispered of a love I never knew.

I also felt a peace that I know only comes from you.

I rest in your comforting arms and in them, I will reside.

For only in them am I truly alive.

Arms of Grace

Corrupted and stained, I wish to see the light of day again.

There are many ways to avoid the pain

in the places that I've been.

Then I saw a light piercing through the darkness,

shining so true and bright.

But I cowered back, thinking that

you wouldn't love me anymore.

But You opened your Arms of Grace

And brought me back into the fold.

Lord, I am so unworthy of You!

Falling down into the filth that is my life,

You came running to my side.

I look up. Are those tears in your eyes?

Holding me to your chest, You rock me gently and say,

"You are precious and honored in my sight.*

My beloved child, welcome back home."

How wonderful is this favor! How beautiful is its sound!

It saved a poor sinner like me.

I was once lost in darkness, but now I'm in the light;

So great is my Savior's love for me.

*Isaiah 43:4

Seeing the Light

Several years have gone by,

having things go my own way.

I don't know what to do;

don't know what to say.

I turned to my friends for help,

but they wouldn't listen.

They left me here all alone.

Now I stumble through the darkness,

trying to find a door.

I look here. I look there.

I look everywhere

for something better than what I'm in.

I found a door,

like golden light.

I want to go there,

and be in the right.

But with all of the sins I've committed,

all the things I've done,

I thought He wouldn't accept me.

Just look at me like I'm no one.

I heard a voice calling,

calling out my name.

I said, "Lord, I'm in shame."

"Come to me, all who are weary and burdened,

And I will give you rest.

I love you and I remember your sins no more."

That sounded too easy,

but I wanted to believe;

To believe that He loves me.

I knelt down with my face to the ground saying,

"You are Lord of Lords and King of Kings.

I want to live with you for eternity."

Letter from God

Precious child, you a very rare and unique person.

Rarer than the rarest gemstone.

My love for you goes far beyond your comprehension.

No mind can grasp the depth of my love for you, my beloved.

I have placed you here for a purpose.

Don't live in the past, but don't forget the lessons it has taught you.

Instead, live in the present and think about how you can change your future with what you have learned and keep in step with me.

Don't be afraid to ask for my help because I will give it to you gladly.

When you go through the rough storms of life and it seems like I'm not beside you;

remember that I'm holding you close and crying along with you.

I want you to share with me your pain and your joys.

I am closest to you in the trying times, my friend.

When you feel lonely when you feel blue,

Remember that I love you and I'm right beside you!

Renewed Hope

Several years have gone by

living in sin and torment.

Guilt and shame are my constant companions

as I walk through this thing called life.

Losing all hope of changing,

I carry the heavy burden of my past.

I'm at the point of breaking

and giving up on everything I have.

But you shined your light in my deepest darkness,

whispering to me of a love I never knew.

Of a life free of guilt and shame.

Of my hope being renewed.

Never have I felt this free.

Not until I met you.

Nothing will ever compare to the hope renewed by you.

Where You Always will be

I look back on my life

and see the blessings you have given me.

You are always there,

even when I cannot see.

I continue on the path you have laid out before me.

Wherever I am Lord,

is where you always will be.

No matter what life throws at me,

you are always there by my side,

guiding me through the fight and

to the victory.

No matter what may be the tide,

you pull me back up just in time!

Lord that is where you always will be.

Every time I fall down on my face,

you hear every cry I raise.

You never leave my side.

I will praise your name!

Beautiful to Me

I've found a place of quiet rest.

This is where your peace finds me.

Only you truly know the troubles that I face.

I lay all my trophies down.

My pride and the cares that I carry around,

I lay them all down at your nail-pierced feet.

For you fill my life up full of blessings.

So abounding are these that I am blown away.

Your grace that you have given me.

You are so merciful, so beautiful to me.

I carry the burdens that seem so hard to bear.

But with you Lord, I know that you care.

So I'm running to you now,

to you now with these.

For you fill my life up full of blessings.

So abounding are these that I am blown away

Your grace that you have given me.

You are so merciful, so beautiful to me.

You are always there, always there for me.

You give me life every single day.

There's nothing I can do now, except praise your name!

At Ease

Remembering the things I hate,

Remembering all my shame.

I lay on the ground broken and needy.

All the time I should've given to you,

Lord, I hope that I'm not too late.

Why do I keep doubting you

when you pulled me through?

I am like Thomas that needed to see some living proof.

For you alone can see the bigger picture.

While I can only see what is right in front of me.

So Lord, I only ask this of you:

when things are dark and it seems I cannot get through,

put your loving arms around me and put my storm-tossed spirit...

At ease.

Trust in You

Even though I am walking in the temporary darkness,

I know you are standing by my side.

I have no fear because I am safe

underneath the shadow of your wings.

Though the winds may blow and the sea toss me to and fro,

I will trust in you alone.

For you are my refuge and hope.

You are always there, even when I sin.

You wait patiently, and you forgive me

when I repent. You lift me up from the depths of the Earth and

comfort me once again.

You are forever the same, nothing will ever change you!

Oh Lord my God,

I will fully trust in you!

Sea of Faces

A sea of faces; that is what I see.

Faces that are lost and searching.

Who will tell of the good news of Christ?

These are the reasons why I fight.

I'm fighting for the hurting, so that they may be comforted.

Fighting so that they can gain a freedom that is eternal life with Christ.

I fight for the blind, so that they can see.

I'm fighting for the hopeless, so that they may have joy and peace.

I fight for the wanting, so that they may experience God's unconditional love.

I will fight not with a physical sword, but with the word of truth.

I will show them compassion in everything I do.

I will not bow down to compromising beliefs,

but instead showing them the light of Christ that is in me.

I will stand up for what I believe, even if I fall,

for I know that I cannot win them all.

I live for Christ and dying to myself daily is gain;

So I raise my hand and say:

"Here am I Lord! Send me!"

Nail Scarred Hands

The nail-scarred hands of Jesus,

are the ones sustaining me.

Those callused carpenter's hands

have set this captive prisoner free.

Oh to be washed white as snow!

To be loved unconditionally!

Who am I but a sinner

that you have extended your hand to me?

Who am I? I am yours! I am the child of the King.

Who is the Lord of Heavenly Armies?

The great I AM.

You are my victory.

Lover of my Soul

Oh, lover of my soul, how well you know me!

You knew that I would break your heart, but still, you pursued me.

You know everything there is to know; I can't hide anything from you.

You know my strengths and weaknesses, when I rise and when I go to bed.

Like a doe searching for water, my soul longs for your touch and voice.

For only you can satisfy the desires of my heart.

Only you can fill the void that is there.

How awesome are your creations!

How beautiful is your work!

The sunrise and sunsets cry out your beauty.

And to think you created them for me. Just for me!

And the sound of thunder! Oh, I'm forever in awe!

For it shows your magnificent strength.

Nothing is impossible for you!

My heart leaps when it hears your voice;

it craves your touch, my lover.

I long for the day you come back.

To take me home so I can be with you for eternity.

Beautiful

Beautiful are the days that are sunny.

Beautiful is the rain that falls upon this dry and thirsty ground.

Beautiful are the lilies of the valley.

Beautiful are your creations that I see.

But more beautiful is the Rose of Sharon;

More beautiful is the love that you have given.

For you have made me into the likeness of your image.

You breathed life into me and I am constantly forgiven.

Salvation is only found in you; thank you, Lord

for leading me to the truth.

Hint of Heaven

I look at the clouds above and see your beautiful majesty.

I see the colors of your rainbow and see the beauty of the King.

I see the variety of colors stretched across the sky.

I can't help but wonder...is this what Heaven is like?

Is the golden light shining on the clouds above

the doorway to your kingdom?

Is the rainbow a pathway to the pearly gates?

Are the clouds painted pink on your tabernacle?

Will the angels dance and sing

or will they stand in awe of your glory?

Will our loved ones be waiting for us to welcome us home?

Will we be gathered around the apostle's feet,

hearing their stories that went untold?

There are more questions I want to ask;

more questions I would like to understand.

If this is what a hint of heaven is like,

I want to be there in the end.

Forever by your Side

Caught in the midst of sin, I am convicted from within.

That my life is not my own, but it was bought at a price.

A price that I can never repay, yet I am saved

by mercy and grace.

Not because of the good things I've done,

but because of who you are.

So I lay down my pride,

asking for forgiveness.

And I remember the reason why you came.

You came down from glory,

to save a poor wayfaring soul like mine;

to spend forever by your side.

When I see a Cross

I think of the one who died for me.

So holy and so pure,

I am in awe of the grace and mercy he has given me.

When I see a cross,

I see one who made my very being.

He knew I would break his heart

And still, he created me.

What a miserable person that I am!

I am humbled he is still with me!

Even when I try to do things on my own,

He still helps me to my feet.

There is no one greater than he;

no animal or manmade thing.

You are mighty to save!

You alone are worthy of my praise!

You Love me anyway

Every breath I take

I long for you to know.

But words are not enough to describe

the love that you have for me.

You are forever faithful God.

You hold me close to your heart.

When everything is falling apart,

you, Lord, are not.

How can I describe what words cannot express?

You came down to Earth and died for me.

Left the splendor of your throne;

you came to set me free.

Though I am unworthy of your love,

and though I fall down time and time again.

You know my thoughts and my heart

And you love me anyway.

I am Yours

Many times I've failed you.

Many times I have been unfaithful.

Many times I've fallen down,

but you still pick me up off the ground.

Many times I have given up.

Many times I have tried to do it on my own.

Many times I ran away from you,

but you haven't given up and are waiting for me to

come home.

What have I done to deserve your attention?

I fall down to my knees,

for your overwhelming love

washes over me.

I am in awe of you, God.

You are all I will ever need

in this life that I have called my own.

To you be all the glory.

To you be all the praise.

I rest now at your feet

because I am yours and at peace.

You see my Future

I am going through a storm that seems to have no end.

I have lost faith and have lost the way.

I am so tired of this

Lord! I am giving you all control.

Please lead me out of this storm

and lead me home.

I want to see the angels dance and sing;

their praises to you who have made all things.

I want to see my loved ones

and tell them everything.

I want to see the face of Christ and forever sing praises to you, my King.

You point me in the right direction

when I have been led astray.

You see my future

when I only see today.

I Want to Love You

When I first laid my eyes on you,

who knew you would be the one for me?

I couldn't believe it was true,

when you married me.

When we have our fights,

I want to make it up to you.

Because baby, you're the only one

I want to spend with for eternity.

I want to dance.

I want to love.

I want to give thanks to the Lord God above.

With all of my heart

and with all of my soul,

I want to spend the rest of my life with you.

I want to love you, baby.

I want to love you.

When we walk towards the setting sun.

When we pass through the pearly gates.

I want to fly with you forever,

forever on white wings.

A Parent's Words

Even though I have moved on,

I am proud of the person you've become.

I have taught you everything I have learned,

ever since your life had begun.

I may not be there to watch your children grow,

to laugh, to cry, or to touch a loved one's hand.

But I will be watching you

until it's your turn to come home again.

Do not grieve for me for long,

but cherish the memories we have shared.

I will be waiting for you at the pearly gates,

with open arms and a smile on my face.

A Grandfather's Love

A grandfather's love can fill up valleys;

he protects everyone he loves and cares about.

His hands are those of a hard worker,

Firm, but gentle when guiding his grandchildren.

His laughter brightens up a day.

It is music to the ears of those about him.

He teaches his children to do what's right,

and they see the wisdom in his eyes.

His voice sings praises when he speaks about the Lord.

His thoughts are set upon the Lord.

He perseveres for the goal that awaits him.

His feet walk in the path of the righteous.

He knows where he is going at the sunset.

Experience

When life runs you over,

don't give up!

Fight back until it's over!

For all the experiences you face

makes you the person you are today.

You can either let the experiences tear you down,

live in them and never let them go,

or learn from them and grow.

It can be hard to let go of the memories,

whether good or bad.

But they are baggage that prevents you

from flying to new heights.

The past is the past

and the future is unknown.

That is why they call this the present.

The Park Bench

I was sitting on a bench in a park one day,

looking forlorn and feeling dismayed.

Reflecting back on the past, I couldn't help but wonder

if what I knew now would help me back then.

Far off into the distance, a lady walked towards me.

She wore casual clothes and had a face that was plain.

She looked healthy with a purple scarf around her lean neck.

Blue eyes with blonde hair and lips that were pink.

"May I sit by you? I am out of breath. You look kind of down; can I help you with this?"

I patted the spot beside me and with a sigh, I said, "I'm sure no one would understand, but why not try?"

She placed her hands in her lap and turned towards me saying, "Speak, for I am listening."

I started, "If I knew then what I know now, I could have saved myself from a lot of heartaches. A lot of consequences I could have avoided; a lot of pain and hurt that I wouldn't have caused.

If I knew then what I know now, oh, what different results there would have been! I would have stayed away from those types of guys, been a little friendlier to those people that I just brushed on by. My life would've been different then!"

I paused and looked over at her, wondering what she was thinking, to see if she smirked. She was still listening, eyes sparkling, with a smile on her face. Oh, what a beautiful smile she had!

"What are you smiling for? What do you think? Are you going to say that I shouldn't think like this?"

She looked at me and said, "I would not say that you are childish, but I would like for you to listen and think."

She paused and fiddled with something on her jeans like she was gathering her thoughts and thinking.

"If you knew then what you know now, you wouldn't have listened; you would have given it a frown. You would have brushed it on by, thinking you knew everything. That they didn't apply to you; how would they know about my pain?

If you knew then what you know now, you wouldn't have understood it like you do today. You wouldn't be you. For the consequences and trials you went through shaped you into who you are today. You wouldn't be the loving and caring person that people love today.

For life is a journey that we all walk upon; each of us learning the same things in different ways on different walks. What you learn today, someone may learn years from now. And what someone learned years ago, you are learning now."

She put her hand gently on my knee and said to me lovingly,

"Dear, God loves you right where you are, but he loves you too much to keep you right where you are. He is patient and loving too. He will wait for you, all the while he will guide you through."

I asked, "Ma'am, how do you know these things? You look about my age if not seven years older."

She smiled and with a cheerful laugh said, "Dearest heart, I was once just like you."

We sat and talked for a while until the wind turned chill and we departed like best friends. That was the last time I saw her; when wisdom came to that park bench.

58619493R00036